# THE POWER OF PUPPETS

## Stories to share with children at KS1 and KS2

### By Georgia Thorp
#### Foreword by Jenny Mosley

## Illustrations by Mark Cripps

LEARNING THROUGH PUPPETS

Acknowledgements
Firstly, I would like to say a big thank you to Jenny Mosley for encouraging me and supporting me in the writing of this book. I would also like to extend my thanks to Ros Bayley, who invited me to one of her workshops and introduced me to the world of puppets and storytelling, and to Ros Grogan who helped me shape the stories at the beginning. Lastly, I would like to thank all the children who have enjoyed watching the puppets tell their stories.

I would like to dedicate this book to Jennifer, Zoë, Nicholas and Ashley.

The puppets in this book are featured with the kind permission of Folkmanis-Puppets.

Cover photographs by Anne Poole.

**Positive Press**

Published in 2005 by:
Positive Press Ltd
28A Gloucester Road
Trowbridge
Wiltshire BA14 OAA

Telephone: 01225 719204
Fax: 01225 712187
Email: positivepress@jennymosley.co.uk
Web site: www.circle-time.co.uk

Text © Georgia Thorp
Illustrations © Mark Cripps

ISBN 1-9048660-3-4

*Printed by:*

HERON PRESS
19-24 White Hays North
West Wilts Trading Estate
Westbury
Wiltshire BA13 4JT

# Contents

## The stories

I first met Georgia seven years ago in a hot, noisy room at London University where I was running an in-depth seven-day course on my Quality Circle Time model. Georgia immediately caught my attention because she quietly radiated enthusiasm for new ideas and a deep commitment to her role as a governor at her local primary school. My respect for Georgia deepened when I met her again on the same course the following year. She had come back to uncover any of the ideas she might have let slip the first time round! I was so impressed by her dedication that I resolved, one day, to ask her to join my team of consultants.

My own passion for puppets was shaped by my relationship with a young boy I worked with as class teacher in an inner London special school. This boy was an elective mute; he had chosen not to speak outside of his home and was receiving weekly psychotherapy sessions at a local children's hospital. After a year he invited me to join in these sessions. I met his exceptionally talented psychotherapist who showed me just how powerful puppets can be. I watched in amazement as this deeply withdrawn boy would whisper his anger, hopes and fears - but only through the voices of hand-held puppets. Months later, he was able to find his voice by giving informal puppet shows at school. It was a long, complex psychological process but this boy was eventually enabled, albeit tremulously, to speak with his own voice to his classmates and teachers.

Inspired by his courage and a huge excitement for the power of puppets, after further training and lots of practical arts experiences, I wove the use of puppets into my developing circle time model.

Children have the ability to suspend disbelief for puppets so that their characters become intensely real and their interactions meaningful. They willingly enter into dialogues with the puppets that they do not commit to adults. Directly from their hearts they proffer wonderful advice and ideas.

In my book *More Quality Circle Time* (1998) I wrote a chapter of puppet scripts for two little animals called Salt and Pepper. I also talked about an experience I had when working with a circle of six- to fourteen-year-olds in a special school in Essex. During their hour-long circle session I introduced a range of games, parachute activities, drama and puppets. At the end of the session, I asked the children what they liked best. One tough older lad muttered, 'The puppets'. When I asked why, he simply said quietly, 'Happy endings, innit?' In other words, although these children had difficult lives, they had learnt through dialogue with puppets that they were still powerful enough to alter events and change the world for the better. If they can discover this power through their imagination then there is a real hope that they will apply the same power to their own lives and imagine different, better futures.

What Georgia has done in this book is to bring a greater rigour and depth to the whole area of children talking in partnership with puppets. Inspired by the wonderful, sensitive work of Ros Bayley, Georgia has gone on to create a series of compelling stories. They act as a safe foundation block from which children can move into philosophy and critical thinking. Her unique, direct and understated style guarantees that they will be fully engaged in a journey of empathy, moral discussion and creative problem-solving. This book will act as a turning point for many children and teachers who are learning how to learn together. I am proud to offer it as a way to revolutionise your circle time, PSHE, RE, citizenship and critical thinking lessons.

**Jenny Mosley**

For the past five years I have worked in many schools, supporting staff and children in developing the Quality Circle Time Model. My passion for puppets began when I attended a storytelling and puppet workshop delivered by Ros Bayley, a wonderfully talented woman. I can remember walking into the room where a group of 12 early years practitioners were sitting in a circle. I felt very self-conscious at the thought of having to 'perform' with the puppets and I was worried about looking silly. I just wanted to sit quietly, listen to Ros and go away with the handouts and try things out in the privacy of my home or in a class where no other adults were present.

Fortunately, my fears were quickly dispelled and soon enough every adult in the room had a puppet sitting on their lap. There was something so powerful and real about the puppets which enabled all of us to believe and empathise with their characters. There were even some sad goodbyes when people parted with their puppets at the end of the day.

The following day, I was speaking to a Headteacher in a school that I worked in. I told her about the workshop with such enthusiasm that when I had finished, she looked at her watch and said, 'Right, can you come into nursery with me and tell the children one of the stories? Their teacher has just phoned in sick and I'm waiting for a supply teacher to arrive'. To be honest, I felt a bit sick. I just wanted to talk about the workshop, I wasn't ready to try it! What if it didn't work and I looked stupid?

The school had a large puppet called Molly which sat in the Headteacher's office but was very rarely used. I looked at Molly and felt scared. I wasn't ready to risk it. In my bag I had a finger puppet and I decided to use that. I walked into the nursery. The children were sitting on the carpet. I took the finger puppet out and put it on my trembling finger and started to tell one of the stories that I had heard the day before. To my relief and delight, the children were keen to hear the story and the little finger puppet held their attention. They answered the questions at the end of the story and they were interested and engaged. This was all I needed to confirm my belief in the power of using puppets for telling a story and it gave me the confidence to continue. I have never looked back.

## *About the book*

This book contains fifteen stories about two fictional characters, Sam and Gloria, who are best friends. Their stories have been developed in Circle Time sessions over the past year and reflect everyday situations to which children can relate. The stories have themes about friendships, feelings, sharing, getting on with others, low self-esteem, school routines and safety.

They are aimed at Early Years/Key Stage 1 and 2 and can be told as part of a Circle Time session or at story time. Each story stands alone; they can be read in any order or chosen to suit a particular situation and they are perfect for telling with puppets.

When young children start to listen to stories, they are taking their first steps towards becoming successful readers. It is by listening that they first become aware that they can become immersed in lives that are not their own and they quickly learn that stories are filled with all sorts of tensions that are sorted out one way or another in the end.

As they are read more and more stories, children learn to anticipate what will happen next. But they often need to learn to check for evidence and build on what they already know. When they are told stories in which the characters encounter problems, they also learn how decisions are made and then they can think about the consequences of actions and apply them to their own lives.

Sam and Gloria face problems that will be familiar to young children. Sometimes the characters make decisions that create problems and then they have to find a way of making things right. In other stories, the problems stem from the behaviour of other people and the character has to work out what to do about it. Often they need help so they have to find someone who will put things right and they have to know how to ask for the help they need.

The questions posed during and at the end of each story are designed to make these skills easier for young children to grasp. The questions can also act as a guide for class discussions about the issues that each story raises. At the end of each story, there are some key phrases which can be used as prompts if you prefer to tell the story without the script and want to focus more on the actions and movements of your puppet. Ideas for follow-on work are also included.

# How to use the puppets

Large puppets have real character and children relate to them very well. You may already have your own puppets which you may want to use. Just use their names in the stories instead of the characters' names.

Using puppets for the first time can be a bit daunting, but once you have practised a few times it will become second nature. Here are a few tips to help you:

- Practise at home. Sit in front of a mirror so you can see what the puppet looks like. Try out different emotions such as happy, sad, tired, angry, shy.

- Sit the puppet on your lap, upright, not slumped.

- Make sure the puppet is able to make eye contact with the children to help them focus and engage with it.

- Use one hand to move the head and the other to work the hand. (I find that if you are right-handed it is easier to manipulate the facial movements with your right hand.)

- Puppets do not need to move all of the time; small movements are very effective.

- You don't need to move the puppet's mouth continuously; at the beginning and end of a sentence is enough.

## Where to store the puppets

The puppets you use for your stories should only be used by adults and they should be treated as if they are very special. Bring them out when you tell a story and put them away when you have finished. Decide on where they will live. This could be in a basket, a bag or in a cupboard. Some classes have a puppet which has its own seat and takes part in Circle Time, while others have a special place where the children can go and speak to the puppet. Remember, if you choose to have puppets sitting in your class, make sure the children are clear about what they can and can't do with them. If you want the children to be able to use puppets, then invest in some finger or hand puppets or make some of your own.

## Introducing the puppets

When you introduce Sam or Gloria for the first time, tell the children that you have someone in the bag or box who would like to tell them a story. Explain that everyone has to be very quiet before they will come out. Carefully and slowly bring out the puppet and sit it upright on your lap.

If you are using Sam, put one of your hands in his head and the other in one of his hands. Put his head down as if he is shy and ask the children what they think is the matter with him. The children will probably tell you that he is shy or that he doesn't know anyone. They will empathise with him immediately and understand what it feels like to be in a place where you don't know anyone.

Ask if the children have any ideas about how to make Sam feel a bit happier. They will make suggestions such as 'Everyone say their name', 'Sing him a song', 'Read him a book' and so on. Choose one of these suggestions; the most usual one is to go round the circle inviting each child to say their name. Manipulate Sam gradually so that he looks up and waves or puts his thumb up. By the end, position him so that he is looking at the children and is much happier and ready to begin the story. I remember in a Year 5 class a girl suggested that they sing him a song. It was so moving, I was close to tears. Sam enjoyed it as well!

## Telling the stories

Before you read a story to the children, it's worth reading it through a couple of times on your own to familiarise yourself with it. Alternatively, use the key phrases at the end of each story as prompts so you can tell the story in your own words and concentrate on working the puppet.

Included in the stories are open questions which allow the children to be more actively involved in the telling of each story. For example, in *The school trip to the zoo*, the children are asked what Sam can see out of the coach window. There is no wrong answer to this question - accept all of the children's suggestions. It is up to you whether you go on to say what Sam actually saw, incorporating some of the things which the children said.

Another example is from *Sam goes to the farm*, when the children are asked to suggest what fruit Sam might choose for the picnic. Although the story goes on to say that he took an apple and a banana, there is no reason why you cannot change this to something suggested by the children. Incorporating the children's suggestions can help to hold their attention and encourages them to feel that they are really involved in the story.

You may also wish to stop the story before reaching its conclusion and ask the children what they think might happen. Listen to all their ideas and then finish the story. When I first started telling stories with puppets, I would often leave the story open-ended and listen to the children's thoughts about what had happened.

But I have found since that, even when children have told you their thoughts, they still want to know what 'really' happened.

As you become more confident at telling the stories with the puppets, you will begin to develop your own style. There is no 'right' way. You can:

- Tell the story with the puppet making small actions and movements and occasionally giving them a voice.

- Tell the story in the first person, giving the puppet a voice.

- Have a silent puppet who sits on your lap while you tell the story.

Remember, as long as the puppet is sitting upright on your lap and looking at the children, they will engage with it and this allows you to tell the story in a way that is comfortable for you.

You only need to use one puppet at a time, although if you want to you can have the other puppet sitting on a chair nearby. Personally, I find this is a distraction for me as well as the children as they are often tempted to touch or squeeze the puppet or they try to get as close to it as possible. Children don't need to see the other character involved in the story; they will be able to imagine them.

Occasionally, and this does not happen very often, a child will stop listening to the story and start chatting.

Rather than stop the flow, you can use the puppet very effectively to tell them to be quiet. Use the puppet to point to the child and put his finger on his lips to show them that they must be quiet.

## Developing the characters

At the end of the stories, there are suggestions for writing and drawing activities to develop the themes and issues raised. You may also wish to create a:

## Scrapbook

Put the work in a Gloria and Sam scrapbook and keep it in the book or home corner so the children can enjoy it.

## Picture book

Make picture books about each story. The children can make a storyboard or draw pictures and write about how the characters are feeling and what they are doing.

## Photo album

Take photographs of Sam and Gloria in various settings - in the playground, sitting at the table and so on. Put them in a photo album with questions about the photos which link them to the children's own experiences. For example, What does Sam do at playtime? What do you do at playtime?

Above all, have fun using the puppets and telling the stories!

# Sam goes to the farm

Sam was very excited. It was a lovely warm day. The sun was shining and he was going on a trip to the local city farm with his mum. This was Sam's favourite place to visit. He had been to the farm lots of times. He loved seeing all the farm animals.

Sam and his mum were going to take a picnic. He helped his mum make some peanut butter sandwiches and some cheese sandwiches and then he chose some fruit from the fruit bowl on the kitchen table.

> **Which fruit do you think he might have chosen?**
> Sam chose a banana and a big green apple. Bananas and apples were his favourite fruit.

> **What drinks might they have taken?**
> They packed a bottle of water and a carton of orange juice.

The last things they packed were two big slices of chocolate fudge cake. Sam loved chocolate fudge cake. They put all the food and drink into two rucksacks, a big one for his mum and a little one for Sam to carry, and off they went. Sam held his mum's hand very tightly as they walked to the bus stop to wait for the bus.

When the bus came, they got on and paid the bus driver. He gave them a ticket from his machine and they climbed up the stairs and sat right at the front and looked out of the window.

> **What do you think they could see out of the window?**
> They could see people and cars, lorries, shops and more people.

After a while, Sam said, "Are we there yet?"
His mum said, "It won't be long."
A little later, Sam said, "I'm hungry, can we have our picnic now?"
His mum said, "Sam, you have only just had breakfast. We are nearly there. I think this is our stop."
Sam rang the bell and they waited for the bus to stop. They climbed down the stairs carefully and got off the bus. Sam held his mum's hand very tightly while they crossed the road and went into the farm. There were lots of animals at the farm.

> **What animals do you think they saw?**
> They saw pigs and sheep and a cow and ducks and chickens.

Sam was having a great time wandering around the farm looking at all the animals with his mum.

**What sounds do you think they could hear?**
They could hear the sheep baa-ing and the chickens clucking and the pigs snorting.
They could hear children laughing and people talking.

**What do you think they could smell on the farm?**
They could smell the hay and the chickens.

When they had walked all around the farm, they found a bench in the shade and took out their picnic.

**Can you remember what they had taken with them?**
They had some peanut butter sandwiches and some cheese sandwiches, a banana and a big green apple. They also had a bottle of water, a carton of orange juice and some chocolate cake.

As Sam was eating his peanut butter sandwich, a chicken came up to him. Sam gave the chicken a little piece of his sandwich. Just then, his mum's mobile phone rang and she answered it. It was his Auntie Androulla. That meant his mum was going to be talking for a very long time.

He gave the chicken another piece of his sandwich and the chicken ate it and then started to walk off. Sam's mum was still on the phone and Sam felt bored, so he got up and started to follow the chicken. The chicken started to run and Sam started to run after it and he chased it all around the farm. Sam got a bit tired and turned around to go back but... oh no! He couldn't remember which way to go and he couldn't see his mum anywhere. He started to panic and shouted, "Mum, Mum," and people turned and looked at him. Just then, he saw his mum running towards him. She threw her arms around him and Sam tried to explain what had happened.

**What do you think his mum said?**
She said, "Remember Sam, you must never, ever wander off on your own" and she hugged him very tightly.

Sam had learned his lesson and he was never going to wander off again.

# Questions and ideas for follow-on work

**Comprehension**

1. What animals did they see at the farm?

2. What did Sam have for lunch?

**Finding evidence**

1. Why did Sam chase the chicken?

2. Do you think that Sam had a good day or a bad day?

**Identifying feelings**

1. How did Sam feel when he thought he was lost?

2. How did his mum feel?

**Problem solving**

1. What did Sam do when he realised that he was lost?

2. If Sam wanted to go somewhere, what should he have said?

3. Could his mum have done anything to stop him wandering off?

**Sharing experiences and feelings**

1. Have you ever been lost?

2. What happened?

3. How did you feel?

**Follow-on work**

1. Draw or write about a time when you were lost.

## Key phrases for retelling the story in your own words

- It was a hot day. Sam was going to the farm with his mum.

- They made a picnic and took a rucksack.

- Sam held his mum's hand when they went to the bus stop.

- They got on the bus.

- They arrived at the farm and saw the animals.

- They heard and smelled different things.

- They ate the picnic.

- The mobile phone rang.

- Chicken came over to Sam.

- Sam fed the chicken and followed it.

- Turned around and couldn't see his mum.

- Started to panic and shouted "Mum, Mum".

- Mum came running over.

- Sam never wandered off again.

## The special assembly

All the children in Gloria's class had been practising their class assembly for two weeks. They were all going to show something. Some were going to read poems, some were going to show pictures they had painted, some were going to sing songs and Gloria and another girl called Meena were going to do a dance all on their own.

Gloria loved dancing and she had made up a dance to a song she really liked. She practised every day at school and at home. She danced in the sitting room, in the garden and even in the bathroom. Her mum watched her and said, "You're going to be brilliant, Gloria."

The assembly was the next day and Gloria started to feel very nervous.

> *Why do you think she was feeling nervous?*
>
> She thought she might forget the steps or she might trip and fall over and the other children might laugh at her.

That evening, she said, "Mum, I don't want to do the dance."
Her mum could see she was nervous and said, "Gloria, you've been practising for weeks, it's alright to feel a bit nervous but you'll be fine and I will be there watching you."
Gloria still wasn't happy. She started to panic and said, "Please don't make me do it, please don't, it's too scary, please don't."
Her mum gave her a big hug and said, "Gloria, don't worry. When we go in to school tomorrow we'll have a word with your teacher, Miss Wilson, and if you really don't want to do it then you don't have to."

That night, Gloria went to bed with her favourite little monkey, Ralph, and told him how she felt. She eventually fell asleep, cuddling Ralph very tightly.

> *What do you think she said to Ralph?*
>
> She told Ralph she was feeling very nervous because she might forget the steps or she might trip and fall over and the other children might laugh at her.

When she woke up the next morning, her tummy felt all funny. She was still worried about the assembly. When they got to school, Gloria and her mum went to speak to Miss Wilson.

Miss Wilson listened to Gloria's mum and then she looked at Gloria and said, "You've worked ever so hard and we are all very proud of you." Then she said something that surprised Gloria. She said, "To tell you the truth, I always get nervous when I have to do an assembly in front of the whole school. I worry that I might make a mistake or forget something but once I start it's alright and I begin to enjoy it, so I understand how you are feeling. Why don't you go and have a chat with Meena? She's doing a dance and she's feeling a bit nervous as well." So Gloria went off to find Meena.

> **How do you think Gloria was feeling now?**
> Gloria felt a bit better.

Gloria and Meena talked for a few minutes and then Gloria went back to Miss Wilson and said, "We have an idea. Meena and I would like to be on stage at the same time. I can wait for Meena and she can do her dance and then she can wait for me to do my dance."

Miss Wilson thought that this was a very good idea, so Meena danced first and Gloria stood in the corner of the stage and watched her. When it was Gloria's turn, she looked around for her mum. She saw her sitting at the back and she waved at Gloria. Gloria's heart was beating very fast as she performed her dance. When she finished, everyone clapped and then the whole class came back on stage and took a bow and everyone clapped again. Gloria felt very proud.

# Questions and ideas for follow-on work

## Comprehension

1. Where did Gloria practise her dance?

2. What was special about today?

3. What is the name of Gloria's friend?

## Finding evidence

1. Why was Gloria feeling nervous?

2. Why did Gloria cuddle Ralph tightly when she went to bed?

## Identifying feelings

1. How was Gloria feeling when she talked to Ralph?

2. Who can show me how Gloria felt before the dance?

3. Who can show me how she felt afterwards?

4. What did Miss Wilson do to try to make Gloria feel better?

## Problem solving

1. What did Gloria and Meena decide to do?

## Sharing experiences and feelings

1. Have you ever been nervous about doing something?

2. Can you describe how it felt?

3. What helped you?

4. Who can you talk to if you're feeling nervous or worried?

## Follow-on work

1. Draw or write about a time when you felt nervous.

2. Draw or write about Gloria performing her dance in assembly.

- Class assembly.

- Everyone was doing something.

- Meena and Gloria were going to perform a dance each on their own.

- Gloria practised at school and at home.

- She practised in the sitting room, in the garden and in the bathroom.

- The day before assembly, she started to feel nervous.

- She talked to her mum.

- Talked to Ralph, her favourite little monkey, and told him how she felt.

- Next morning, Gloria's tummy felt funny.

- Mum and Gloria went to school and talked to Miss Wilson.

- Gloria talked to Meena.

- They decided to be on the stage at the same time.

- Meena danced first.

- Then it was Gloria's turn.

- Gloria looked for her mum in the audience and her mum waved to her.

- Gloria did her dance.

- Everyone clapped.

- All the class came back onto the stage and took a bow and everyone clapped.

- Gloria felt very proud.

## Sam is special

Sam woke up one morning feeling very sad. He got up slowly, had a wash and got dressed. He went downstairs to the kitchen for his breakfast. He put his favourite crunchy cereal in his favourite blue bowl and poured on some cold milk. He sprinkled on a little bit of sugar, but not too much. His mum said too much sugar was bad for his teeth. His mum poured him a glass of orange juice and said, "Is something the matter, Sam? You don't look very happy."

Sam just shook his head and said in a very sad voice, "No, nothing's the matter, but do I have to go to school today?"

His mum said, "Are you sick, Sam?"

"No," said Sam.

"Well," said his mum, "you can't have a day off unless you are sick."

So Sam finished his breakfast, put on his coat and off they went to school.

When they got to the school gates, his mum waved goodbye and Sam walked into the playground. He looked around and saw his best friend, Gloria. She came over and said, "Hello Sam, what's the matter? You don't look very happy, what's wrong?"

Sam looked down at the floor and said, "Nothing's wrong."

But Gloria said, "I can see that there's something wrong, please tell me."

Sam took a deep breath and said, "Alright, I'll tell you as long as you don't laugh at me."

"Of course I won't laugh at you," said Gloria.

"Well..." said Sam. "You know John is good at sports..."

"Yes..." said Gloria.

"I'm not," said Sam shaking his head. "And you know Sofi is good at maths..."

"Yes..." said Gloria.

"I'm not," said Sam, shaking his head. "And you know Mustafa is good at drawing cars and colouring them in..."

"Yes..." said Gloria.

"I'm not," said Sam shaking his head. "And you know Paul is good at just about everything and he's always getting stickers..."

"Yes..." said Gloria.

"I never get stickers," said Sam. "I'm not good at anything."

Gloria thought for a moment and then she said, "You are good at things, Sam."

Sam looked at Gloria and said, "What am I good at?"

Gloria said, "Well, remember last week, when I fell over and hurt myself? You looked after me. You could have carried on playing but you didn't, you stayed with me all playtime and told me jokes and made laugh. That was a very kind thing to do."

"Oh," said Sam. "What else am I good at?"

"Well..." said Gloria. "You are brilliant at looking after your guinea pigs, Fudge and Dandelion. You keep their hutch clean and you give them fresh hay every day. You give them fresh water to drink and you chop up their carrots and cucumber into little pieces. And you brush their coats so that they stay healthy and you put them out in their run every morning."

Sam said, "Yes, I suppose I am good at those things but I didn't think those things mattered."

Gloria looked at Sam and said, "Everything we are good at matters."
Do you know what? Sam felt much happier and said, "Later on
I'm going to draw a picture."

*What do you think he drew a picture of?*
He drew a picture of Fudge and Dandelion sitting in their hutch
eating carrots, with Gloria standing next to them with a big smiley face.

## Questions and ideas for follow-on work

### Comprehension

1. What did Sam have for breakfast?

2. Can you remember the name of one of the guinea pigs?

### Finding evidence

1. What is Sam good at?

2. How does Sam look after his guinea pigs?

3. How do you think Gloria knew that he wasn't very happy?

### Identifying feelings

1. How did Sam feel when he thought about the other children in his class?

2. How did he feel after his chat with Gloria?

### Problem solving

1. What did Sam say when Gloria asked him to tell her why he was looking so unhappy?

2. What did Gloria do to make him feel better?

### Sharing experiences and feelings

1. Have a round of "I am good at..." during Circle Time.

### Follow-on work

1. Draw the picture you think Sam drew later in the day.

2. Write some kind words and pictures that can be used to make people feel good and make a wall display of them.

- Sam woke up feeling sad.

- Got up slowly, had a wash, got dressed and went down for breakfast.

- Had his cereal, a little bit of sugar and cold milk in his blue bowl and a glass of orange juice.

- Sam didn't want to go to school.

- Mum asked if he was sick but he wasn't.

- Sam put on his coat and went to school.

- Mum waved to him at the school gates.

- Gloria asked Sam what was wrong.

- Sam said nothing at first then he told her.

- John is good at sports.

- "I'm not," said Sam.

- Sofi is good at maths.

- "I'm not," said Sam.

- Mustafa is good at drawing cars and colouring in.

- "I'm not," said Sam.

- Paul is good at everything and is always getting stickers.

- Sam said he wasn't good at anything.

- Gloria told him he looked after her when she fell and hurt her knee and was very kind.

- She also told him that he was good at looking after Fudge and Dandelion, his guinea pigs, and gave them hay and chopped up their carrots and cucumber into small pieces and gave them fresh water.

- Sam didn't think that counted.

- Gloria said everything we are good at matters.

- Sam felt happier and drew a picture.

# Gloria's new glasses

Gloria was going to visit the opticians.

**Who can tell us what this means?**
The opticians is a place you visit to have your eyes tested.

Gloria had been finding it hard to read the writing on the board in class so she was going to have her eyes tested. She was feeling worried because she hadn't been to the opticians before and didn't know what would happen. She asked her mum if it was going to hurt. Her mum told her that it wouldn't hurt and there was no need to worry.

When they got to the opticians, Gloria sat in a special chair and the optician covered one of Gloria's eyes with a small piece of card and asked her to read out the letters from a large poster on the wall. Some of the letters were big and some were small.

Gloria found it very easy to read the letters and when she had finished, the optician said, "Well done, Gloria. That was very good."

Then she covered Gloria's other eye. Gloria found it much harder to see the letters. She could read the very big letters but she couldn't read the little ones. The optician said that Gloria would need a pair of glasses to help her to see better. She could choose the frames she wanted now but she would have to wait two weeks before she could collect them.

The optician brought out some glasses for Gloria to try on and a mirror for her to look in. She tried on lots of different pairs. It was a bit strange looking in the mirror wearing glasses. Gloria felt like she was looking at someone else. She couldn't decide which ones she liked best. Her mum picked up a blue pair and said, "How about these?" Gloria tried them on and looked in the mirror, then she said, "Yes Mum, these are the ones I want."

Two weeks seemed like a very long time to wait. Gloria was very excited when they finally went back to the opticians to collect her new glasses. The optician put them in a special case so they wouldn't get broken.

When they got home, Gloria put on her glasses to show her gran. Her gran thought she looked very smart. Gloria kept them on for the rest of the day and even went to bed wearing them. "Oh, Gloria," said her mum, smiling, "You don't need to wear them all the time, only for reading." Gloria took them off and put them very carefully in the special case and went to sleep.

At school the next day, Miss Wilson asked the children to get out their reading books. Gloria opened her book bag and took out her book and put on her glasses. Sam thought they looked really cool. Gloria felt very happy. She kept her glasses on when she went out to play. In the playground, she saw a boy called Mohammed who was in her class. He was pointing at her and laughing, saying, "Four-eyes, four-eyes!"

Gloria felt very upset. Sam told her to ignore him but she couldn't. She took off her glasses, threw them onto the ground and ran away. Sam picked them up and followed Gloria. He couldn't find her so he went over to Miss Wilson who was on playground duty. When Sam told Miss Wilson what had happened, she was very cross.

After playtime, the children returned to their classroom. Miss Wilson asked Gloria to take the register to the office and called Mohammed over to her desk. She said, "I hear you've been saying unkind things to Gloria about her new glasses." Mohammed looked at the floor. Miss Wilson continued, "In our class, we try to be kind to each other. Gloria wears glasses to help her to see better.

I think she looks nice in them. Lots of people have to wear glasses. How would you feel if people made fun of you for something you were wearing?"

It went very quiet and Miss Wilson asked Mohammed and the rest of the class what they could do to make Gloria feel better. When Gloria came back to class, Miss Wilson said, "Mohammed has got something he'd like to say to you."

> **What do you think he might have said?**
> He said, "I'm really sorry that I called you names. I didn't mean to upset you. I won't do it again."

Then one girl said, "I like your new glasses. They really suit you."
Another boy said, "Sometimes people tease me about my red hair but I take no notice."

Miss Wilson smiled at Gloria and gave the glasses back to her. Gloria put them on and sat down next to Sam to do some work.

# Questions and ideas for follow-on work

## Comprehension

1. Where did Gloria get her glasses from?
2. Where did Gloria keep her new glasses?
3. How long did she have to wait to get her new glasses?

## Finding evidence

1. How do you know that Gloria was pleased with her new glasses?
2. Why did Mohammed call her names?

## Identifying feelings

1. How did Gloria feel when she first got her glasses?
2. How did she feel when Mohammed called her names?
3. How did she feel when the children said kind things to her?

## Problem solving

1. What did the children say to make her feel better?
2. What did Miss Wilson do to help Gloria?

## Sharing experiences and feelings

1. Has anyone ever made fun of you because of something you were wearing or the way you look?
2. How did you feel?
3. What did you do?

## Follow-on work

1. If someone comes in to your class with a new haircut or is wearing a new pair of glasses, think about what you can say to make them feel good.
2. Write or draw about something you remember from the story.

## Key phrases for retelling the story in your own words

- Gloria was going to the opticians to have her eyes tested.

- She sat in a special chair.

- The optician covered one of Gloria's eyes and she had to read the letters on a large board.

- She read the letters very well.

- Then the optician covered the other eye and Gloria found it much harder to read the letters.

- The optician said she could choose some glasses to help her see better.

- Gloria tried on lots of glasses and chose a blue pair.

- She had to wait two weeks before she got them.

- Gloria wore them all day and went to bed in them.

- The next day, Gloria put them in her book bag.

- At school she put them on.

- Sam thought they looked cool.

- At playtime, Mohammed called her "four-eyes" and she was upset.

- She threw her glasses on the ground and ran away.

- Sam picked them up and told Miss Wilson what had happened.

- In class, Miss Wilson sent Gloria to the office with the register.

- Miss Wilson talked to Mohammed.

- Mohammed apologised to Gloria when she came back.

- Other children said nice things to her.

# Sam has chicken pox

Sam had chicken pox. He couldn't go to school. He couldn't go to the park. He couldn't have Gloria over to play in case she caught it. He had to stay at home until he got better. His mum had taken a few days off work to look after him.

She had been up most of the night pouring Sam drinks of water when he needed them and making sure he wasn't scratching his spots. Now it was morning and Sam was in the sitting room, lying on the sofa and wearing his stripy blue pyjamas. His teddy bear, Jacob, was lying next to him. His mum had brought down his duvet, the one with pictures of boats, seashells and fish on it. She had covered Sam up so that he was warm and snug.

Sam's mum was busy in the kitchen doing some washing and ironing. Sam was watching television and began to feel thirsty. He called out, "Mum, I need a drink of water." His mum brought him a glass of water. A few minutes later, Sam began to feel hungry. He called out, "Mum, can I have some soup?" His mum brought him a bowl of chicken soup and Sam ate it. He searched through the television channels, but there was nothing he wanted to watch. He called out, "Mum, there's nothing on TV, can you put a video on?" His mum came back into the room and went to the shelves to get a video and she put it on for him.

A few minutes later, Sam was bored with the video. He called out, "Mum, I've seen this video before. Can I do some drawing instead?" His mum came back into the room carrying his drawing things. Sam decided to draw a picture for Gloria. After a while, he needed to sharpen his pencil. "Mum," he called, "I can't find my pencil sharpener." His mum came back into the room and had a quick look around. She picked up the sharpener from where it had fallen. "Here you are, Sam," she sighed.

Sam sharpened his pencil and carried on drawing. When he had finished he called, "Mum, I've finished my drawing, what can I do now?" He waited but his mum didn't come. "Mum, I'm bored, what can I do?" he called again.

Still his mum didn't come. Sam got up off the sofa, grumbling to himself. He pulled the duvet round his shoulders and dragged it with him through to the kitchen. "Mum…" he started to say, but when he got into the kitchen he saw his mum sitting at the table with her head on her arms. She was fast asleep.

Sam realised that his mum must be very tired as she had not had much sleep the night before. He remembered how she had looked after him and made sure he was comfortable and had everything he wanted. He looked at the pile of ironing she had been working on. She had been busy all morning while he had been lying on the

sofa but she had never been too busy to come and give him the things he had asked for. Sam realised that he had forgotten to say "please" and "thank you" and he felt very ashamed.

Just then, Sam's mum woke up and yawned. Sam went over and gave her a big hug. "Goodness," said his mum. "Did I fall asleep?"
"Why don't you go and lie on the sofa?" said Sam. "I'll make you a cup of tea."
"Thank you, Sam," said his mum, with a smile.

## Questions and ideas for follow-on work

### Comprehension

1. Who can remember something that Sam made his mum bring him?
2. Why did Sam's mum fall asleep?

### Finding evidence

1. Have any of you got some ideas about why Sam's mum was feeling so tired?
2. Why did Sam feel ashamed?

### Identifying feelings

1. Who can show me how Sam's mum looked when she was tired?
2. Who can show me how Sam looked when he found his mum asleep in the kitchen?

### Problem solving

1. What did Sam do to show his mum that he was sorry?
2. What else could Sam have done to show his mum that he was grateful?

### Sharing experiences and feelings

1. Who looks after you when you are not feeling well?
2. How do you show that you are grateful?

### Follow-on work

1. Make a card from Sam to his mum, thanking her for looking after him.

- Sam had chicken pox.

- He couldn't go to school or the park and Gloria couldn't visit him.

- His mum took time off work to look after him.

- She had been up during the night pouring him drinks and making sure he wasn't scratching his spots.

- In the morning, Sam laid on the sofa in the sitting room.

- His mum brought him his duvet and covered him up.

- She was busy in the kitchen and Sam kept calling out.

- First he was thirsty.

- Then he wanted some chicken soup.

- Then he wanted to watch TV and then a video.

- He asked to do some drawing and lost his pencil sharpener.

- His mum came in and found it.

- Sam called his mum to ask what he could do next.

- She didn't come.

- Sam grumpily went to see where she was and found her asleep in the kitchen.

- Sam felt ashamed when he realised how busy his mum had been.

- When Sam's mum woke up, Sam offered to make her a cup of tea.

- Sam's mum smiled.

# Sam goes back to school

Sam was going back to school. He had been at home all week with chicken pox. He was looking forward to seeing his teacher and the rest of his class, but most of all he was looking forward to seeing his best friend, Gloria. He had drawn seven pictures for her and he couldn't wait to give them to her.

> **What pictures do you think he might have drawn for Gloria?**
> He drew pictures of himself and Gloria playing together and smiling, and pictures of his guinea pigs, Fudge and Dandelion.

He folded up the pictures carefully and put them in his book bag. He skipped to school with his mum. When they arrived at the school gates, he waved goodbye to her and ran off to find Gloria. Sam looked all around for Gloria and then he saw her playing with someone by the shed, right at the other end of the playground. Sam shouted "Gloria!" and ran over to her. Gloria was too busy playing and didn't hear him. Sam ran over, shouting, "Gloria, Gloria I'm back!"

Gloria was playing with a boy whom Sam had never seen before. They both stopped and looked at Sam. "Hello Sam," said Gloria. Then she whispered something to the boy and they both ran off, laughing.

Sam didn't understand why Gloria had run off. He felt very upset and had to bite his lip to stop himself from crying. Just then, he heard the school bell ring and he slowly walked over to his teacher, Miss Wilson, who was waiting for the class to line up. Miss Wilson said, "It's lovely to see you, Sam. I hope you're feeling better. We've all missed you."
Sam put his head down and stood very quietly.

When they got to class, everyone sat down for quiet reading time. Gloria sat next to her new friend and Sam sat on his own. Miss Wilson came over to speak to Sam. "What's the matter, Sam?" she asked.
Sam kept his head down and said in a very quiet voice, "Gloria has found another best friend and she doesn't want to be my friend anymore."

Miss Wilson said, "Would you like me to have a word with Gloria?"
Sam thought for a minute and then said, "Yes please."

Miss Wilson went to speak to Gloria and told her how Sam was feeling. Then she brought Gloria over to where Sam was sitting. Gloria said, "You left me all on my own and you were away for ever. I thought you were never going to come back and

I didn't have anyone to play with. George started school last week and I looked after him and now we are friends."

Sam took the pictures that he had drawn for Gloria out of his book bag. He handed them to her and said, "These are for you."
Gloria looked at the pictures and said, "Thank you, Sam. These are brilliant."
Then she said, "I'll see you at playtime" and she went back to her seat.

# Questions and ideas for follow-on work

## Comprehension

1. What is the name of Sam's teacher?
2. What did Sam take to school to give to Gloria?

## Finding evidence

1. What might make you think that Sam is good at art?
2. How do you know that Miss Wilson is a kind teacher?

## Identifying feelings

1. How did Sam feel when Gloria and George ran away from him?
2. How do you think Gloria felt when Sam was away for so long?

## Problem solving

1. Gloria missed Sam when he was away. Who can tell me what she did so that she wouldn't be quite so lonely?
2. What did Sam and Gloria do to put things right?

## Sharing experiences and feelings

1. Have you ever been away from school and things were different when you came back?
2. What happened?
3. What did you do?
4. How did you feel?

## Follow-on work

1. Draw a picture or write about what you think happened at playtime.
2. Discuss what sometimes happens with your friends at playtime.

## Key phrases for retelling the story in your own words

- Sam was home all week with chicken pox.

- He was looking forward to seeing Gloria.

- Sam drew seven pictures for her.

- He went to school.

- He looked around for Gloria.

- Sam saw her with a boy he didn't recognise.

- He went to say hello.

- Gloria and the boy laughed at him and ran off.

- The bell went for start of school.

- Sam lined up.

- His teacher was pleased to see him.

- Sam was very upset.

- In class, his teacher asked Sam what was the matter.

- Sam told her.

- His teacher spoke to Gloria.

- Gloria told Sam she had been lonely and helped look after the new boy.

- Sam gave her the pictures he had drawn.

- Gloria liked them.

- Gloria said she would see him at playtime.

# Gloria and the lake

It was a hot, sunny day. Gloria and her mum had arranged to meet Sam and his mum in the park, close to the lake. Gloria helped her mum to make some sandwiches to take with them.

> **What sandwiches do you think they made?**
> They made some cheese and pickle and some egg sandwiches.

They packed the sandwiches in a sandwich box and took some cold drinks from the fridge and Gloria's mum put it all in a bag.

> **What drinks do you think they took?**
> They took two cartons of orange juice with straws and a bottle of cold water.

Gloria had a special blue tartan picnic blanket which she carefully folded and put into her little rucksack and they set off for the park. Gloria skipped happily all the way there. As soon as they arrived, Gloria spotted Sam running towards her and she started to jump up and down with delight.

Sam and Gloria ran ahead while their mums chatted behind them. They stopped under a huge oak tree and Gloria took out the blanket. Sam helped her lay it out and they both sat down.

When the grown-ups caught up with them, Sam and Gloria helped take out the food and drink and some little paper plates and cups from the bags. They placed them in the middle of the blanket so they could all share.

> **What do you think Sam and his mum might have brought?**
> Sam's mum had brought some grapes, cheese, crisps and some delicious homemade cheese and tomato pizza.

"Yummy," said Gloria. Cheese and tomato pizza was her favourite. They all helped themselves to the food. When they had finished, Gloria asked if she and Sam could go down to the lake and feed the ducks with the left over bread and pizza crusts. Both mums said they could as long as they didn't wander off. They were to be very careful near water and come straight back after they had fed the ducks. Gloria and Sam collected all the bread and pizza crusts and raced over to the lake.

On the water there was a beautiful white swan and a duck swimming around with her ducklings. Sam and Gloria broke the bread and pizza crusts into little pieces and threw them into the water. They had such good fun watching the ducks and the swan dipping their beaks into the water to find the food. Sam threw the last piece of bread in and they were just about to head back when Gloria spotted a long stick on the ground and picked it up.

Sam said, "Come on, we have to go back," but Gloria wasn't listening. She was concentrating on pushing the stick down into the bottom of the lake to see how deep it was. She kept pushing the stick as far as she could and lifting it out again. When she pulled the stick out, it was covered in dirty, brown sludge.

She handed Sam the stick and said, "You have a go." Sam refused at first but it did look like fun so he took the stick and swished it around in the water. Gloria noticed an empty can floating on the water. She was worried that the ducks might get their beaks stuck inside, so they tried to get the can out of the water using the stick. The can floated further and further away. Gloria stretched her arm out as far as she could and tried to get the can to float towards her by swishing the stick in the water.

Suddenly, she lost her balance and fell into the water with a loud splash. Luckily, it wasn't very deep and she managed to stand up. She was covered from head to toe in brown sludge. The water was quite cold and she started to shiver. Sam told her to grab hold of his hand and he pulled her out.

Sam helped Gloria walk back in her dripping wet clothes to where their mums were. "Oh my goodness!" cried Gloria's mum. Sam explained what had happened. Gloria's mum said, "I told you to be sensible and never do things that could be dangerous. You could have been badly hurt or even drowned. You are very lucky that Sam was there to help you out of the water. Now, promise me that you will never do that again."

Gloria's mum took the picnic blanket and wrapped it round Gloria to keep her warm. Gloria was really sorry and had learned her lesson.

## Questions and ideas for follow-on work

### Comprehension

1. What did Gloria do wrong?

2. What did her mum say about feeding the ducks?

3. Why didn't Gloria listen to her mum?

4. Why didn't she listen to Sam?

### Finding evidence

1. What was Gloria's favourite food?

2. What made Gloria fall into the water?

3. Why did her mum wrap her up in the blanket?

### Identifying feelings

1. How did Gloria feel when she saw the can floating on the water?

2. How did Gloria feel when she fell into the water?

3. How did Sam feel when Gloria fell into the water?

4. How did Gloria feel when she got out of the water?

### Problem solving

1. Why was it dangerous?

2. What did Sam do to help Gloria?

### Sharing experiences and feelings

1. Have you ever done something dangerous?

2. What happened?

3. How did you feel?

### Follow-on work

1. Find out what the safety rules are in your school and at home and draw or write about them.

2. Draw pictures or write about why we have safety rules.

- Gloria, Sam and their mums were meeting in the park.

- They all made a picnic to take.

- Gloria took the blue tartan picnic blanket.

- They met Sam and his mum in the park.

- They ate their picnic.

- Gloria asked if they could feed the ducks and the swan.

- The mums said they could as long as they were careful.

- They fed the ducks and turned to go back.

- Gloria found a stick in the water and started playing with it.

- Gloria tried to get a can out of the water with the stick.

- Gloria slipped and fell in.

- Sam helped her out and took her back to their mums.

- They told their mums what had happened.

- Gloria's mum wrapped her up in the blanket.

- Gloria learned her lesson.

Freddie lived opposite Sam. They often used to play together after school. One afternoon they were both playing in Freddie's garden. Freddie told Sam that he was going to be moving to a new house very soon. Sam didn't want him to go. He said, "I don't want you to go, you're my friend." But Freddie had to move because his dad had got a new job that was far away.

One Saturday morning, a few weeks later, Sam woke up and could hear lots of people talking outside. He got out of bed and looked out of the window. He saw a big removal van parked outside and there were lots of people carrying boxes and furniture from Freddie's house and loading them into the van. Sam watched for a very long time and then he saw them carry Freddie's train set into the van. Sam felt sad and he went downstairs to look for his mum. He found her sitting in the kitchen having a cup of tea.

She could see that Sam looked upset and asked, "Are you alright, Sam?"
Sam started to cry and said, "Freddie's going and I won't see him again."
Sam's mum got up and gave him a big hug and said, "Why don't you make Freddie a card and take him some chocolate when you go over to his house to say goodbye?"

Sam thought that was a good idea and he sat at the kitchen table to make a card for Freddie. He drew a picture of himself and Freddie playing in the garden and he wrote, 'Dear Freddie, I will miss you. From Sam' and then he drew a smiley face.

Sam's mum kept some treats in a large tin on top of the cupboard. Sam reached for the tin and carried it carefully to the kitchen table and looked inside.

*Can you guess what was in the tin?*
There were chocolate bars, biscuits and lollipops.

Sam picked out two chocolate bars, one for Freddie and one for himself, and went around to Freddie's house. Freddie's mum told Sam that Freddie was in the garden so Sam went to find him. Freddie was sitting on the grass watching two snails eating a leaf. Sam sat down next to him and handed him the card and one of the chocolate bars. Freddie opened the card and read it out loud. 'Dear Freddie, I will miss you. From Sam.' Freddie said, "Thank you, Sam."
They ate their chocolate bars and watched the snails. After a while they heard Freddie's mum call out, "Time to go now Freddie!"
Sam and Freddie got up and walked to the front of the house. Freddie's mum smiled

at Sam and gave him a hug and Freddie said, "I'll write to you, Sam."
Freddie and his mum got into their car and Sam and his mum waved to them as they drove away.

## Questions and ideas for follow-on work

### Comprehension

1. Where did Freddie live?

2. What did Sam make for Freddie?

3. What was Freddie doing in the garden?

### Finding evidence

1. Can you think of something that Sam will miss doing with Freddie?

2. How do you know that Sam and Freddie are good friends?

### Identifying feelings

1. How did Sam feel when he saw the removal van outside Freddie's house?

2. How did Sam feel when he made a card for Freddie?

3. How did Freddie feel when Sam gave him the card and present?

### Problem solving

1. Who gave Sam the idea of making a card?

2. What did Freddie say to make Sam feel OK?

### Sharing experiences and feelings

1. Have you had a friend who has moved away or gone to another school?

2. What was it like?

3. How did you feel?

4. Have you ever moved house or school?

5. What was it like?

6. How did you feel?

### Follow-on work

1. Discuss whether Freddie will write to Sam.

2. Write a letter from Freddie to Sam.

3. Write a letter from Sam to Freddie.

4. Write a letter or draw a picture to a friend who has moved away and tell them some of your news.

- Freddie and Sam lived next door to each other.
- Freddie was moving away because his dad had a new job.
- Sam felt sad because Freddie was his friend.
- His mum told him to make a card and take some chocolate to Freddie.
- Sam drew himself and Freddie playing in the garden and wrote 'Dear Freddie, I will miss you. From Sam' and drew a smiley face.
- Sam took the card and chocolate and found Freddie in the garden watching two snails eating a leaf.
- Sam gave Freddie the card and they ate the chocolate.
- Freddie's mum said it was time to go.
- Freddie said he would write.
- Freddie and his mum got into their car and drove off.
- Sam and his mum waved to Freddie and his mum.

# The shiny new tractor

Gloria had just come back from the shops with her mum. She was sitting on the sofa in the sitting room holding a small blue box. Inside the box was a shiny new blue tractor with big silver wheels and a farmer sitting in the driver's seat with a little black dog. Gloria had been saving up her pocket money for weeks. Finally she had saved enough money to buy it.

She had invited Sam around to play with her farm and she couldn't wait to show him her new tractor. She stood at the window and jumped up and down impatiently until she saw him walking up the garden path. She ran to her front door and opened it and held out the tractor for Sam to see.

"Wow, this is really cool," said Sam, taking the tractor. He took the farmer out of the seat and patted the dog. They raced into the sitting room and Gloria and Sam tipped out the box of farm toys and made a big farmyard and put all the animals inside. They spent ages arranging the animals around the farm and Gloria used the tractor to carry bales of hay.

Sam was desperate to play with the tractor and he asked if he could have a turn because Gloria had been playing with it for ages. Gloria didn't want to let him play with it. She said, "It's brand new and I haven't played with it properly yet."

Sam felt upset. He only wanted to play with it for a little while, so he said, "Why don't we take it in turns? I'll take the tractor up to the farm and around to the pigs and you can take it over to the cows." But Gloria didn't want to.

Sam thought this wasn't much fun and said he wanted to go home. Gloria couldn't understand why he wanted to go home and said he was jealous, just because he didn't have a tractor.

Gloria said she was thirsty and went to the kitchen and brought back two cartons of orange juice. She gave one to Sam and drank the other one herself. She decided to drive the tractor to where the cows were but she couldn't find it. "Have you seen the tractor, Sam?"
"No," said Sam.
"Well, where is it?" asked Gloria.
Sam shrugged and said he didn't know.

Gloria asked Sam to help her look for it. He looked under the sofa and the cushions but it wasn't there. Gloria noticed something sticking out of Sam's pocket. "Sam," she said, "what's that in your pocket?"

Sam looked down sheepishly at his pocket and pulled out the shiny new blue tractor with the farmer and the little black dog. "I was just borrowing it," he said innocently.

"You were stealing it," said Gloria.

"I wasn't stealing it. You didn't let me play with it and I just wanted a go. I was going to give it back," said Sam.

Gloria reached out and tried to snatch the tractor off him but Sam threw it across the room and said, "Take your stupid tractor then."

Suddenly they heard a voice saying, "What's going on here?" They looked up to see Gloria's mum. Sam felt very ashamed and stared down at the ground. Gloria's mum knelt down beside him and asked him what had happened.

"She wouldn't let me play with it," he said, with tears trickling down his face.

"Is this true?" said her mum looking at Gloria.

"Yes," said Gloria, "but he tried to take it home."

Gloria's mum looked at them and said, "You two are best friends, you shouldn't fall out over a toy."

Sam swallowed hard and said, "I just wanted to play with the tractor, I wasn't stealing it, honest. I'm really sorry."

Gloria's mum said, "Have you got anything to say Gloria?"

Gloria felt sorry for Sam. Maybe she had been a little selfish so she said, "I'm sorry, I should have let you have a turn."

Sam went over to where he had thrown the tractor and picked it up. He handed it to Gloria.

> **What do you think Gloria did next?**
> She took the tractor and said, "Shall we carry on playing with the farm?"
> Sam said, "Yes," and they spent the rest of the afternoon playing nicely together and sharing the tractor.

# Questions and ideas for follow-on work

## Comprehension

1. What was in the small blue box?
2. Who came to play with Gloria?

## Finding evidence

1. How long had Gloria been saving up for the tractor?
2. Why do you think she couldn't wait to show it to Sam?
3. What did they do with the farm animals?
4. Why didn't Gloria let Sam play with the tractor?
5. How did Gloria know that Sam had taken the tractor?

## Identifying feelings

1. How did Gloria feel when Sam asked to share the tractor?
2. How did that make Sam feel?
3. How did Gloria feel when Sam threw her tractor across the room?
4. How did Gloria feel when her mum spoke to her?

## Problem solving

1. Who helped them to sort out the problem?
2. How did they share the tractor?

## Sharing experiences and feelings

1. Have you ever taken something that wasn't yours?
2. What happened?
3. Have you ever argued about a toy with your friend?
4. What happened?
5. How did you feel?

## Follow-on work

1. Think of as many ways as you can to show how Gloria and Sam shared the tractor and draw a picture or write about it.

## Key phrases for retelling the story in your own words

- Gloria had saved up her pocket money to buy a new toy.

- It was a shiny new tractor with a farmer and his dog.

- Sam was coming to her house to play.

- When Sam arrived, Gloria showed him the tractor.

- Sam thought it was really cool.

- They played in the sitting room with the farm animals.

- Sam wanted a turn with the tractor.

- Gloria didn't want to share because it was new and she hadn't had a proper go.

- Sam wanted to go home.

- Gloria got some orange juice from the kitchen.

- When she returned she couldn't find the tractor.

- Sam helped her to look for it.

- Gloria saw the tractor in Sam's pocket and accused him of stealing.

- Sam got upset and threw the tractor across the room.

- Gloria's mum came in and talked to them.

- Gloria and Sam apologised and Sam gave the tractor back.

- They played nicely together for the rest of the afternoon.

## Sam has school dinner

Sam always took a packed lunch to school but he wanted to try having school dinners. His friend Gloria told him that school dinners were really nice and so he asked his mum if he could try them. Gloria said she would show him what to do but just before the bell went for dinner, Miss Wilson sent her on an errand. She wasn't back in time, so Sam found himself in the dining hall all on his own.

Well, he wasn't on his own exactly. There were lots of other children from his class but they were all having packed lunches and they sat in a different place. Sam was very nervous and his heart was beating fast. He watched the boy in front of him take a dinner tray from a pile. He did the same. He waited patiently in the dinner queue.

The hall was very noisy. It was giving Sam a headache. Children were chatting loudly with their friends and making clinking noises with their knives and forks. Sam looked around to see if Gloria had come in for dinner yet but he couldn't see her anywhere.

The queue moved quickly. Soon he was at the front. He could see a tray of cheese and mushroom pizza and a tray of broccoli quiche. He wanted pizza but the dinner lady served him a large slice of quiche. He didn't like quiche but he was too shy to say.

He moved along the line and another dinner lady asked him what vegetables he wanted. He was still busy looking at the quiche on his plate and before he could say anything, she had put a large scoop of peas next to his quiche. He didn't like peas but he was too shy to say.

The next dinner lady asked him if he wanted chips or mashed potatoes but he was too busy looking at the peas sitting next to the quiche and before he could say anything, she gave him a big scoop of mashed potatoes. He didn't like mashed potatoes but he was too shy to say.

He looked at his plate with quiche, peas and mashed potatoes. Then he moved along to the pudding section. The boy in front had the last piece of chocolate sponge. Sam loved chocolate sponge but there was none left and the dinner lady gave him strawberry yoghurt. He hated strawberry yoghurt but he was too shy to say.

> *How do you think Sam was feeling now?*
> He wanted to cry but he gritted his teeth to stop himself.

Sam held his tray very tightly while he looked around for somewhere to sit. He sat down and looked at his dinner - a giant slice of quiche, millions of peas, a mountain of mashed potatoes and a sea of strawberry yoghurt.

> **What do you think he did next?**
> Sam was very hungry. He looked at the food on his plate and a big tear rolled down his cheek.

Just then a voice said, "Sam, there you are!" It was Gloria. Even though she had been just a few places behind him in the line, he hadn't seen her. She sat next to him and asked him what was wrong and he quietly told her what had happened. "Why don't you try a bit of the quiche? I've got some as well," said Gloria.

Sam tried a bit of the quiche. It wasn't too bad and he managed to eat most of it. He felt much happier now that Gloria was with him. Then Gloria said, "Try some of the peas and mash, you might like them." So Sam tried some peas but he didn't like them and he tried some mash and that tasted quite nice so he ate it all. Then he tried the strawberry yoghurt but he didn't like it.

The next day, Sam decided to have school dinners again. Although he still felt very shy, when he got to the front of the line he took a deep breath and said, "Pizza please," in a loud voice.

# Questions and ideas for follow-on work

## Comprehension

1. What did Gloria tell Sam about school dinners?
2. Which did Sam like best, pizza or quiche?

## Finding evidence

1. Why did Sam feel shy talking to the dinner ladies?
2. Why did he want to go into dinner with Gloria?

## Identifying feelings

1. How did he feel when he saw the food on his plate?
2. How did Sam feel when Gloria found him?
3. How did he feel when he tried his dinner?

## Problem solving

1. What could he have said to the dinner lady?
2. What did Gloria do to help Sam?
3. What did Sam do the next day so that he could get a piece of pizza?

## Sharing experiences and feelings

1. Have you ever felt too shy to ask for something in school?
2. What was it?
3. What did you do?
4. Have you ever tried eating something different?
5. What was it?
6. Did you like it?

## Follow-on work

1. Do some role play where you practise asking for things in a loud voice and saying please and thank you.
2. Who can you speak to if you are feeling shy?
3. Who can help you?

## Key phrases for retelling the story in your own words

- Sam was going to try school dinners.
- Gloria said they were nice.
- Gloria was going to help him at the counter.
- Gloria was sent on an errand so Sam went to lunch on his own.
- Sam followed the boy in front of him.
- When it was Sam's turn to choose his food, he felt very shy.
- The dinner lady gave him quiche instead of pizza.
- She gave him mash instead of chips.
- She gave him peas.
- There was no chocolate sponge left and he had to have strawberry yoghurt.
- Sam felt upset.
- He found somewhere to sit and started to cry.
- Gloria found him.
- Sam told her what had happened.
- Gloria told Sam to try some of the food on his plate.
- Sam managed to eat some of it.
- Sam felt much happier.
- Next day he was still shy but asked the dinner lady for pizza in a polite but loud voice.

# The tea party

Gloria's favourite toy was a little monkey called Ralph. He was very soft and cuddly and Gloria loved him. Every night, before she went to sleep, she would talk to Ralph and tell him things.

*What do you think she might have said to Ralph?*
That evening she was telling Ralph that they would have to get up early the next morning because her best friend, Sam, was coming around and they were going to have a tea party with Ralph and Jacob and then they were going to hunt for treasure in the garden.

*Can you guess who Jacob was?*
Jacob was Sam's favourite teddy bear.

Jacob had accidentally fallen into the washing machine when Sam was much younger and when he came out some of the stuffing was missing from his leg and one of his button eyes had fallen off. So Sam had wrapped a bandage around his leg and had drawn the missing eye on his face.

In the morning, Gloria got ready for her tea party. She had a red china tea set which was a present from her granddad. She opened the box and took out the red teapot, four red cups and saucers and four big red plates. Ralph helped her arrange them neatly on the little red table in the sitting room. Then they put four red chairs around the table.

She filled the teapot with orange juice and put a chocolate biscuit on each plate. When Sam and Jacob arrived, they all sat down on the little red chairs. Sam and Gloria sat next to each other and chatted and so did Jacob and Ralph.

Sam poured the orange juice from the teapot into the little cups and they pretended they were drinking cups of tea. When they had finished their biscuits they ate Ralph's and Jacob's biscuits too because Ralph and Jacob weren't very hungry.

Sam and Gloria decided to leave Ralph and Jacob sitting on the little red chairs while they wandered out into the garden to begin their treasure hunt. Gloria found a bucket and two spades, which they used to dig up some mud as they explored for hidden treasure. It wasn't long before they discovered some old coins and a rusty keyring. They put them in the bucket and carried on digging until they found a ring and a necklace that Gloria had lost ages ago. She squealed with delight when she saw them.

They worked very hard making the hole bigger and bigger and they didn't realise how late it was getting. Sam's mum arrived to take Sam home. Gloria begged Sam to stay a bit longer but Sam's mum said it was time for Sam to go to bed.

Gloria sulked when Sam left and went inside to find Ralph. She started to tell him all about the treasure they had found but then she noticed Jacob, still sitting on the red chair. "Oh no!" she cried. "Sam has forgotten Jacob and he won't be able to sleep without him. We'll have to go round to Sam's house."

But Gloria's mum said, "It's very late, you'll have to look after him and tomorrow you can take him to school and give him to Sam."
Gloria started to cry. She knew that Sam was going to be very upset because he never went to bed without Jacob. She thought how she would feel if she had forgotten Ralph. She picked up Jacob and looked at him and said, "I know you'll be lonely without Sam but I promise I'll look after you."

That night, she took Ralph and Jacob to her room. She put some pyjamas on Ralph and found a spare pair for Jacob and tucked them both up in bed. She thought about Sam and she hoped he would be alright.

The next day, Gloria got up really early. When it was time to leave for school, she carefully put Jacob into her school bag. When she got to school, Sam was sitting on a bench looking very sad. Gloria rushed over to him, opened her bag and took out Jacob. Sam's face lit up with a big smile as he reached for Jacob. He held him close and whispered something in his ear.

> *What do you think he might have whispered?*
> "I'm sorry I forgot you. I'll never leave you anywhere again."

# Questions and ideas for follow-on work

## Comprehension

1. What was the name of Gloria's monkey?
2. What was the name of Sam's teddy?

## Finding evidence

1. How do you know that Gloria loved Ralph?
2. How do you know that Gloria has a very kind granddad?
3. What treasure did they find in the garden?

## Identifying feelings

1. How did Gloria feel when Sam and Jacob came to her house?
2. How would Gloria have felt if she had forgotten Ralph?

## Problem solving

1. How did Gloria look after Jacob?
2. Why did she get up early the next day?
3. Do you think Sam was allowed to keep Jacob at school?
4. What do you think he did with him?

## Sharing experiences and feelings

1. Have you ever lost something that was special?
2. What happened?
3. How did you feel?

## Follow-on work

1. Draw a picture of Ralph and Jacob.
2. Draw a picture or write about your favourite toy.

- Gloria had a favourite toy monkey called Ralph.

- Sam, her best friend, was coming to her house with his teddy, Jacob.

- They were going to have a tea party and hunt for treasure in the garden.

- Gloria and Ralph put out the red china tea set with four cups and saucers on the red table with four red chairs.

- Gloria filled the teapot with orange juice and put a chocolate biscuit on each plate.

- When Sam and Jacob arrived, they all had a tea party.

- They left Jacob and Ralph sitting on the chairs and hunted for treasure in the garden.

- They found an old necklace and a rusty keyring.

- Sam forgot to take Jacob home.

- Gloria looked after him and put some pyjamas on him and tucked him up in bed with Ralph.

- Next morning, Gloria took Jacob to school in her book bag.

- Gloria saw Sam and gave Jacob to him.

- Sam was happy and whispered something to Jacob.

## Sam's bad day

Sam was fast asleep having a wonderful dream. He was dreaming that it was a hot, sunny day and he was at the seaside. He could hear the sound of the waves crashing against the rocks and he was sitting on the sand with his friend, Gloria, and they were eating ice cream. Sam was just about to lick the strawberry sauce off his ice cream, when he heard a voice shouting, "Sam, Sam, wake up! The alarm hasn't gone off! You're going to be late for school and I'm going to be late for work."

Sam sat up, rubbing his eyes and wondering where he was. When he realised that he was in his bed and not at the seaside, he felt very disappointed. He hated being late for school so he leapt out of bed, splashed some cold water on his face, quickly got dressed and hurried down the stairs. Sam didn't have time for breakfast but his mum gave him a banana to eat on the way. He grabbed his school bag and walked briskly to school with his mum.

When he arrived at the school gates, he found that they were locked so he pressed the buzzer and someone in the office opened the gates for him. He turned around to say goodbye to his mum but she was gone. He didn't even hear her say goodbye. He raced into the school building, up the stairs and into his class just as his teacher, Miss Wilson, called out his name from the register. Sam was out of breath but managed to say, "Yes, Miss."

He quickly sat down at the table he shared with Gloria but she wasn't there. Jack, who was sitting behind, could see that Sam was wondering where she was and whispered, "Gloria's off sick."

The first lesson was maths and Miss Wilson said, "Hands up if you can tell me what 3 x 3 is." Sam put his hand up. "Yes, Sam," said Miss Wilson.
"Six," said Sam. The rest of the class started to laugh at him.
His teacher said, "Good try Sam, but not quite."

It was the wrong answer. Sam was confused. He thought it was adding not multiplying. Miss Wilson asked Jack, who said, "Nine, Miss."
"Well done," said Miss Wilson.
When she asked what 3 x 4 was, Sam thought the answer might be 12 but he didn't want to put his hand up in case he was wrong and the others laughed at him again.

At playtime, Sam was feeling hungry. He had only eaten a small banana and he could hear his tummy rumbling. He sat on a bench in the playground and watched the other children playing.

> **Why didn't Sam play?**
> Sam didn't feel like playing because Gloria wasn't there and he was feeling upset and hungry.

When they were back in class, Sam couldn't concentrate. He spent the whole time thinking about eating the food in his lunch box. He imagined biting his juicy red apple, munching away at his chicken sandwich, drinking his cold water and eating a slice of his mum's delicious homemade chocolate fudge cake.

It felt like hours before he eventually heard the bell for lunch. He put his hand in his school bag and reached out for his lunch box. It wasn't there! Oh, no! He suddenly remembered it was still at home on the kitchen table. He had been in such a hurry that he had forgotten to put it in his bag.

Sam didn't know what to do. He felt too embarrassed to tell anyone so he pretended that his lunch was in his school bag and he strolled out into the playground. He tried to forget how hungry he was and started to play football with Jack, until he accidentally kicked the ball over the fence and Jack called him an idiot. Sam felt angry and kicked Jack really hard on the leg and tried to run off but a dinner lady saw him and Sam had to say sorry.

Sam's day was getting worse. He was hungry, miserable and lonely. He spent the rest of the afternoon sitting at his desk on his own. He refused to do any writing or drawing and he wouldn't listen to the teacher and he didn't talk to anyone.

At home time, he got his school bag and rushed out to the playground where his mum was waiting for him. As soon as he saw her, his eyes filled with tears and his lips quivered. Sam's mum put her arm around his shoulder and said, "Whatever is the matter?" Sam started to sob.

> *What do you think he wanted to say?*
> In between sobbing, Sam managed to say, "Everything's gone wrong today. You left me without saying goodbye. I didn't have any breakfast, Gloria wasn't in school, I forgot my lunch and I'm starving. And I got into trouble. I hate school and I never want to go back."

His mum said, "Oh, dear, it sounds like you're having a really bad day. Let's go home and we'll get you something to eat and you can tell me all about it." She opened her bag and took out a tissue and a packet of crisps and handed them both to Sam. He wiped his eyes and blew his nose. Then he opened the packet of crisps. They were cheese and onion flavour, his favourite. Sam started to feel a little bit better as they walked home.

# Questions and ideas for follow-on work

## Comprehension

1. What was Sam dreaming about?
2. What did he have for breakfast?
3. Why did he forget his lunch?

## Finding evidence

1. What was in Sam's lunch box?
2. Why did he kick Jack?
3. Do you think he was sorry?
4. Can you think of any good things that happened to him?

## Identifying feelings

1. How did he feel when Gloria wasn't in school?
2. How did he feel when Jack called him names?
3. How did he feel when he got the maths question wrong?
4. What made it worse?

## Problem solving

1. When did Sam's day start to go wrong?
2. Can you think of anyone who could have helped Sam?
3. Was there anyone Sam could have spoken to?
4. What would Gloria have said to him?
5. What do you think he did when he got home?

## Sharing experiences and feelings

1. What do you like to eat for breakfast?
2. Can you think of a time when you had a bad day?
3. What happened?
4. How did you feel?
5. Who can you speak to if you are having a bad day?
6. How can we help someone if they are having a bad day?

## Follow-on work

1. Draw a picture or write about the people we can talk to in school and at home if we are having a bad day.

- Sam was dreaming he was at the seaside eating an ice cream with Gloria.
- His mum woke him up to say that the alarm didn't go off.
- Sam felt disappointed.
- He got dressed and had a wash.
- There was no time for breakfast.
- His mum gave him a banana.
- He grabbed his school bag and rushed to school.
- Sam ate the banana on the way.
- When they arrived at the school, the gates were locked.
- Sam got to class just as the register was being called.
- He sat down at his desk but Gloria wasn't there.
- Jack told him that Gloria was off sick.
- Sam answered the maths question wrongly.
- Everyone laughed at him.
- At playtime, he was feeling hungry and he sat on a bench.
- He couldn't concentrate in class.
- At lunchtime, he realised he had forgotten his lunch box.
- He felt too embarrassed to tell anyone.
- Sam played football with Jack.
- He accidentally kicked the ball over the fence and Jack called him an idiot.
- Sam kicked Jack and the dinner lady told him to say sorry.
- Sam refused to do any work in the afternoon.
- At home time, he found his mum in the playground and started to sob.
- He told her about his bad day.
- Mum gave him a tissue and a packet of cheese and onion crisps.
- They walked home.

# Gloria floods the toilets

It was painting time in class. Gloria and Meena were painting a picture together. They painted a picture of themselves sitting in a big boat on the lake, eating ice creams. They painted a big yellow sun in the corner and lots of blue water. When all the children had finished, Miss Wilson took the pictures and spread them out to dry on a big table in the classroom.

Miss Wilson sent two children at a time to the toilets to wash their hands so that they would be ready for fruit time. Gloria and Meena were the last to go. They went to the washbasin, turned on the taps and washed their hands with soap and water. Suddenly Meena said, "Gloria, let's fill the sink up with water so that it will be like the lake in our picture."

Gloria thought it was a good idea, so they put the plug in the plughole and watched the basin fill up with water. Gloria said, "I wonder how high the water will go?" But when the water reached the hole at the top of the basin, it started to disappear down the hole.

Meena said, "I wonder what would happen if we put a paper towel in the hole?" They looked at each other and then Gloria quickly took a paper towel and scrunched it up and pushed it into the hole so no water could get out.

Just then a girl in their class called Jasmine came in and said, "Miss Wilson told me to tell you two to hurry up." Gloria and Meena forgot about the water in the sink and hurried back to class.

They sat down just as Miss Wilson was handing out the fruit. Meena and Gloria loved fruit time.

> **What kind of fruit do you think was there?**
> There were mangoes, bananas, apples, pears and oranges.

The fruit was cut up into small pieces and put in a big blue bowl. Gloria had some mango and pear and Meena had some banana and orange. After fruit time, all the children took out their reading books and read quietly.

Just then Miss Shaw, the Headteacher, came in and spoke quietly to Miss Wilson. Miss Wilson asked the class to stop reading because Miss Shaw wanted to speak to them. The children looked up and Miss Shaw looked very cross and spoke in a very strict voice.

She said, "Someone has flooded the girls' toilets and there's water everywhere. This is a very serious matter. If anyone knows anything about this, please come and see me in my office at playtime."

Gloria and Meena looked at each other. They felt very embarrassed and scared and sat very still. They noticed Jasmine looking at them and whispering to the girl next to her.

At playtime, Gloria said to Meena, "Perhaps we should go and tell Miss Shaw it was us." But Meena said, "No, we'll get into trouble."

After playtime, a message came to say that Miss Shaw wanted to see Gloria and Meena in her office. They left the classroom and walked slowly along the corridor. The last time Gloria had been sent to Miss Shaw's office was when she had done a really good piece of work and Miss Wilson had said she could show it to Miss Shaw. She felt very different this time as she went into Miss Shaw's office with Meena.

Miss Shaw looked at the girls and said, "Do you two know anything about the 'flooding' in the girls' toilets?"
Gloria and Meena looked down at the floor. Then Gloria nodded. She spoke in a very little voice and said, "We didn't mean to do it. We were just playing and we forgot to turn the taps off. I'm really sorry."

> **What do you think happened next?**
> Miss Shaw said it was a shame they hadn't owned up straight away but she was pleased that Gloria had told the truth. They were going to have to stay in her office at lunchtime and if they did anything like this again she would speak to their parents.

# Questions and ideas for follow-on work

## Comprehension

1. What did Gloria and Meena paint a picture of?

2. What did Gloria and Meena do that was really naughty?

## Finding evidence

1. How did Gloria and Meena flood the toilets?

2. Did Gloria know she was doing something wrong?

3. What do you think Jasmine whispered to the girl next to her?

4. How did Miss Shaw know what Gloria and Meena had done?

## Identifying feelings

1. How do you think Gloria felt on the way to Miss Shaw's office?

2. Why do you think Gloria spoke in a little voice in Miss Shaw's office?

3. How do you think Gloria felt about staying in Miss Shaw's office at lunchtime?

## Problem solving

1. Do you think Gloria learned her lesson?

2. What should they have done when Miss Shaw came into the classroom?

3. Why did Gloria decide to tell the truth?

4. What do you think Gloria's mum would have said?

## Sharing experiences and feelings

1. What rules do you have in your school about using the toilets?

2. Can you think of a time when you did something wrong?

3. What happened?

4. How did you feel?

## Follow-on work

1. Draw or write about your favourite part of the story.

- Gloria and Meena were in class painting a picture.
- They painted a lake with blue water and a boat.
- Miss Wilson sent two children at a time to wash their hands.
- Gloria and Meena went last.
- They put the plug in the sink and filled it up with water.
- They blocked the hole with paper towels.
- Jasmine came in and called them back to class.
- They forgot to turn the taps off and went back to class.
- It was fruit time.
- After fruit time they did some quiet reading.
- Miss Shaw came in and spoke to Miss Wilson.
- Miss Shaw spoke to the children and asked if anyone knew about the flooding.
- Jasmine whispered to her friend.
- Gloria and Meena stayed quiet.
- Gloria suggested they owned up but Meena said no.
- After break, Miss Shaw asked to see Gloria and Meena in her office.
- Gloria admitted it was them.
- Miss Shaw thanked her for being honest.
- They had to stay in her office at lunchtime.
- If they did it again, their parents would be told.

## The school trip to the zoo

Sam was very excited. He was going on a school trip to the zoo. His mum made him a packed lunch. In his lunch box he had a chicken sandwich, a chocolate bar, a very big banana, a small carton of orange juice and a bottle of cold water. She gave him a pound to spend in the gift shop.

Sam had been looking forward to this trip for a very long time. His class had been working on a project all about animals in the zoo. He was looking forward to seeing all the animals, especially the giraffes. They were his favourite. He liked to draw pictures of giraffes with long, long necks.

The coach arrived at the school gates and all the children lined up in pairs, climbed onto the coach and sat down. Sam and Gloria sat together and when all the children had put on their seatbelts, the coach driver started up the engine and off they went.

It felt like they were on the coach for a very long time and, after a while, a boy called Jack started to feel a bit sick. Miss Wilson gave him a paper bag to hold just in case he needed to use it. Sam was feeling a bit hungry but his teacher said, "No eating on the coach!" So Sam looked out of the window.

> **What do you think he could see out of the window?**
> He saw buildings, lots of shops and people doing their shopping.

When they arrived at the zoo, the first thing the children wanted to do was eat their lunch but Miss Wilson said it was only 11 o'clock and they had to wait until lunchtime. They walked around and saw lots of different animals. The zookeeper said they could feed the elephants and he gave them some apples to give to them. Jack tried to feed a paper bag to one of the elephants but the teacher caught him just in time and gave him a good telling off.

Finally, they saw two giraffes. "Wow," said Sam. "This is the first time I have seen a giraffe in real life. They're huge!"
There was a mummy giraffe standing with a baby giraffe. All the children said, "Ahhh."

At lunchtime they sat on the grass and ate their lunch.

> **Do you remember what Sam had?**
> He had a chicken sandwich, a chocolate bar, a very big banana, a small carton of orange juice and a bottle of cold water.

Miss Wilson said, "When you finish your lunch, please remember to put your litter in the bin. We don't want to leave any rubbish on the grass."

It was almost time to get on the coach to go back to school but they had one more thing to do - visit the gift shop. All the children went into the shop and started to be very silly and run around until Miss Wilson told them to calm down or they would have to wait outside.

Sam wondered what to spend his pound on. He saw some pencils with different animals on them and one had a picture of a giraffe on it. He reached to take it but Jack picked it up first and took it to the cash desk.

Sam felt like crying but he didn't. He asked the lady at the cash desk if there were any more but the lady said that was the last one. She said there were lots of elephant pencils and monkey pencils but Sam didn't want an elephant pencil or a monkey pencil, he wanted a giraffe pencil. Then in a loud voice, Miss Wilson said, "Time to get on the coach children. Hurry up and buy your gifts."

Sam didn't want to go home with nothing so he took an elephant pencil and paid for it. The lady smiled at him and said, "I think you've made a good choice." She put it in a small paper bag for him. Sam felt a bit disappointed as he walked out of the shop.

Miss Wilson counted all the children when they got on the coach and they set off back to school. All the children were tired but happy, except for Sam.

Suddenly the coach went over a bump in the road and Jack's giraffe pencil slipped out of his bag and rolled over to Sam's seat. Sam looked at the pencil on the floor below him, the pencil that he wanted more than anything. Looking around to check no one was watching, he reached out and picked it up and very quietly put it in his paper bag and then sat very still.

A few minutes later, he heard Jack cry out, "I've lost my pencil! I've lost my pencil!" The children who were sitting close to Jack, including Sam, looked down on the floor to see if they could see it. But they couldn't.

When they got back to class, Jack started to cry again and Miss Wilson said, "Now children we've had a brilliant day, but it seems that someone may have taken Jack's pencil by mistake and I would like everyone to check their bags and see if we can find it." Sam felt embarrassed.

> *What do you think he did?*
> He slowly opened his bag and took out the giraffe pencil. He put his hand up and said, "Is this it?"

Jack looked at it and his face lit up in a big smile and he said, "Yes, yes that's my pencil." Sam handed it over.
Miss Wilson said quietly, "That was very honest, Sam. I know how much you like giraffes."

Sam took out his own pencil with the picture of an elephant on it and thought that even though he had wanted the giraffe pencil, it was better to be honest and not take something that wasn't his. And he began to draw a picture of a giraffe with his elephant pencil.

# Questions and ideas for follow-on work

## Comprehension

1. Who did Sam sit next to on the coach?
2. Who was feeling a bit sick on the way?
3. What did Sam want to buy in the shop?

## Finding evidence

1. How did Sam know that Jack had the giraffe pencil?
2. Why did he give the pencil back?

## Identifying feelings

1. How did Sam feel when he saw Jack was crying?
2. Can you show me how Sam looked when he saw Jack crying?

## Problem solving

1. What did Jack do when he realised that his pencil was missing?
2. What did Miss Wilson do?
3. Was there anything else Sam could have done?

## Sharing experiences and feelings

1. Have you ever taken something that didn't belong to you?
2. What happened?
3. How did you feel?

## Follow-on work

1. Can you think of any other animals you might find in the zoo?
2. Draw or write about your favourite animal.

## Key phrases for retelling the story in your own words

- Sam was excited because he was going on a school trip to the zoo.
- His mum made him a packed lunch.
- His class had been doing a project about animals in the zoo.
- The giraffe was his favourite animal.
- The coach arrived.
- Sam sat next to Gloria.
- They put on their seat belts and set off.
- Jack felt sick and the teacher gave him a paper bag.
- Sam felt hungry on the coach but there was no eating allowed.
- They looked out of the window.
- They arrived at the zoo and wanted lunch but it was too early.
- They looked at all the animals.
- They fed the elephants with apples from the zookeeper.
- Jack gave the elephant a paper bag and was told off.
- Sam saw the mummy and baby giraffes.
- They all sat down and had lunch.
- They went to the gift shop.
- Jack bought the last giraffe pencil.
- Only elephant and monkey pencils were left.
- Sam wanted the giraffe pencil but bought an elephant pencil.
- On the journey home, the coach went over a bump in the road.
- Jack's pencil fell out.
- Sam took it and put it in his bag.
- Jack realised he had lost his pencil and started to cry.
- Children including Sam looked on the floor but they couldn't see it.
- Back in class, the teacher asked the children if they could check their bags.
- Sam gave back the giraffe pencil.
- The teacher thanked Sam.
- Sam thought it was better to be honest.
- Sam drew a picture of a giraffe.

Gloria was getting ready for bed. She brushed her teeth, kissed her mum goodnight and went upstairs to her bedroom. She was very excited because her class was going to have a teddy bears' picnic the next day and she was going to take Ralph.

Ralph was her favourite toy. He wasn't a teddy bear, he was a monkey. But it didn't matter, you could take any soft toy. She tucked Ralph into her bed and said, tomorrow you are going to the teddy bears' picnic so you had better go to sleep now so you can join in all the fun."

Gloria was just about to get into bed when she remembered her farm animals that were in a box under her bed. Gloria thought she would have a little peep and check that all the animals were in the box. She pulled out the box from under her bed and carefully took the lid off and looked inside.

**What animals do you think she had?**
She had pigs, cows, horses and hens.

All the animals were there. Gloria was going to put the lid back on but she thought the animals might like to come out and play for a little while. Soon all the animals were spread out on the carpet and Gloria forgot she was supposed to be tucked up in bed asleep. Instead, she made a sty for the pigs, took the horses for a walk around the farm and milked the cows. She was having so much fun that she didn't even hear her mum come in until she heard a voice say, "Gloria, what are you doing? I came up to make sure you were asleep. It's 10 o'clock."

Gloria looked very guilty and said, "I was just checking to make sure my animals were alright."
Gloria's mum was not very pleased with her and said in a very cross voice, "Get into bed now, you are going to be very tired in the morning." Gloria left the animals on the carpet and got into bed very quickly. She cuddled up to her little monkey and fell fast asleep.

The next morning, Gloria was very tired. She found it very hard to get out of bed and she nearly fell asleep eating her breakfast. Gloria and her mum had to walk to school very fast so that she wouldn't be late and they just managed to get there as the bell went. Gloria kissed her mum goodbye and rushed to her class.

As she walked into the classroom, Gloria looked around and saw all the children holding their teddy bears for the teddy bears' picnic. "Oh no," cried Gloria.

**What do you think had happened?**
It was the teddy bears' picnic and she had forgotten to take Ralph to school. He was still tucked up in bed fast asleep.

Gloria looked at all the other children hugging their teddies and getting ready for the picnic and she started to cry. Sam came over with his teddy bear called Jacob. Jacob was his favourite teddy. He was a very old bear with only one eye and a bandage on his leg.

Sam said, "What's wrong, Gloria?"
Gloria said, "I forgot to bring Ralph. He is still at home in bed and he's going to miss the picnic."
Sam thought for a bit and said, "Why don't you go and see Miss Wilson and maybe you can borrow Jasper the class teddy?"
Gloria was thinking about Ralph still tucked up in her bed. She wished that she had gone to bed early so that she would have remembered to bring him.
"Come on," said Sam," I'll come with you to ask Miss Wilson." So they walked over to Miss Wilson and asked her.
Miss Wilson said, "Of course you can borrow Jasper."

So Gloria took Jasper to the teddy bears' picnic. Although she enjoyed looking after him, she felt very guilty about forgetting Ralph. As soon as she got home, she rushed up to her bedroom and took Ralph out of bed and cuddled him and said, "Ralph, I'm sorry I didn't take you to school today." Then she gave him a big hug and started to tell him about the picnic.

# Questions and ideas for follow-on work

## Comprehension

1. Why did Gloria stay up late?

2. Why did she forget Ralph?

## Finding evidence

1. How do you know that Ralph is Gloria's favourite toy?

2. What did Sam do to help?

## Identifying feelings

1. How did Gloria feel when she walked into the classroom?

2. Who can show me how she must have looked?

3. How did Gloria feel when she took Jasper to the picnic instead?

## Problem solving

1. What could Gloria have done when she went up to her bedroom?

2. What idea did Sam have?

3. What did Miss Wilson do to make Gloria feel better?

## Sharing experiences and feelings

1. Have you ever forgotten something because you were tired?

2. What happened?

3. What did you do?

4. How do you behave when you are tired in school?

5. What time do you go to bed?

## Follow-on work

1. Make a chart of the different times that everyone goes to bed.

2. Draw a picture of the teddy bears' picnic.

3. Write a story about the teddy bears' picnic.

4. Draw a picture of what you think Jasper, the class teddy, looks like.

## Key phrases for retelling the story in your own words

- Gloria went up to bed.

- She was very excited about the teddy bears' picnic.

- Gloria tucked Ralph into bed.

- She took out the farm animals and played with them.

- She didn't realise the time and was still playing at 10 o'clock.

- Mum was very cross.

- Gloria went to sleep.

- Next morning she was very tired.

- She went to school.

- She walked into her class and realised she had forgotten Ralph.

- Sam had brought his teddy, Jacob.

- Gloria felt guilty about forgetting Ralph.

- Sam and Gloria asked Miss Wilson if they could borrow the class teddy to take to the teddy bears' picnic.

- Gloria went home and told Ralph all about it.

- She told him that she would never forget him again.

# Other books in the series...

## Puppets at Large

Puppets as partners in learning and teaching in the Early Years
by Linda Bentley

# Training For Everyone from Jenny Mosley Consultancies

## The Art of Storytelling

Gain insights into how storytelling and story making can contribute to the linguistic, emotional, physical and cognitive development of children.

## The Power of Puppets

Encourage everyone to get their puppets out of the cupboard and use them creatively within the classroom.

*For further details about these and other training courses available from Jenny Mosley Consultancies, visit www.circle-time.co.uk*

To order a catalogue, please contact:

**Positive Press Ltd**

28A Gloucester Road, Trowbridge, Wiltshire BA14 0AA
Telephone: 01225 767157  ·  Fax: 01225 755631  ·  E-mail: circletime@jennymosley.co.uk

---

### Puppets for Peace

International Puppets for Peace Day is celebrated annually around the world and invites everyone to perform a puppet play about peace. This new movement was influenced by Rudolph Steiner who insisted that the use of puppets has the power to heal the ravages of conflict. Last year, plays were performed in the UK, Canada, USA and South Africa. The belief is that even the simplest tale told through and with puppets will extend a circle of peace which will one day extend and hold everyone within it.

For more information, contact: Suzanne@junipertreepuppets.com (US).